Asherah

The Queen of Heaven - Canaanite Magick Book 1
Baal Kadmon

Copyright information

Copyright © 2017 by Baal Kadmon

All rights reserved. No part of this book may be reproduced by any mechanical, photographic, or electrical process, or in the form of a recording. Nor may it be stored in a storage/retrieval system nor transmitted or otherwise be copied for private or public use-other than "fair use" as quotations in articles or reviews—without the prior written consent of the Author.

The Information in this book is solely for educational purposes and not for the treatment, diagnosis or prescription of any diseases. This text is not meant to provide financial or health advice of any sort. The Author and the publisher are in no way liable for any use or misuse of the material. No Guarantee of results are being made in this text.

Kadmon, Baal

Title: Asherah: The Queen of Heaven - Canaanite Magick volume 1

—1st ed

Printed in the United States of America

Cover image: Asherah

Book Cover Design: Asherah

At the best of my ability I have credited those who created the pictures based on the research I have conducted. If there are images in the book that have not been given due copyright notice please contact me at Resheph@baalkadmon.com and I will remedy the situation by giving proper copyright credit or I will remove the image/s at your request.

Dedication

This book is dedicated to The Great Queen of Heaven, Asherah and to my patron Saint, Saint Expedite.

Disclaimer

Disclaimer: By law, I need to add this statement.

This book is for educational purposes only and does not claim to prevent or cure any disease. The advice and methods in this book should not be construed as financial, medical or psychological treatment. Please seek advice from a professional if you have serious financial, medical or psychological issues.

THIS BOOK IS FOR PEOPLE 18 AND OLDER. IF A RITUAL DOESN'T FEEL RIGHT TO YOU, DO NOT PERFORM IT. SOME OF THESE RITUALS ARE NOT SUITABLE FOR ALL AUDIENCES.

By purchasing, reading and or listening to this book, you understand that results are not guaranteed. In light of this, you understand that in the event that this book or audio does not work or causes harm in any area of your life, you agree that you do not hold Baal Kadmon, Amazon, its employees or affiliates liable for any damages you may experience or incur.

The Text and or Audio are copyrighted 2017.

Introduction

Asherah has always enchanted me. I recall when I was young and learning the Jewish faith that much of my Sephardic father's family followed, I remember reading verses from the Bible; more specifically, the Old Testament that would mention her name. It was one of the very first times I encountered the actual names of other Gods in the Old Testament. Instead of being repelled by her, I was drawn to know more about her. I discovered that she was at least as important as the other Canaanite Gods, Baal and El. She is of course, far more than just a Canaanite Goddess.

Canaanite religion has always been interesting to me because it seemed so elusive and dark. The fact that it was in direct opposition to the Hebrew faith gave me a wee bit of satisfaction at the time. What can I say? Sacrilege and Blasphemy started early for me.

In the Bible, we find that the Israelites had many enemies. The two that appear most prominently in the Bible are the Egyptians and the Babylonians. However, I would like to counter that claim. Yes, the Hebrews were enslaved by the Egyptians, at least according to the Bible, and yes, the Babylonians sent the Israelites into a cruel exile which left lasting impressions we still see in modern Judaism to this day. However, the biggest enemy, in my estimation was the Canaanites. I say this for two reasons. Archeologically speaking, it appears that many Israelites themselves were breakaway Canaanites, so it was in their blood so to speak. This is a popular view amongst those who ascribe to the Biblical Minimalist school of thought. I personally, have one foot in Biblical Minimalism myself. Although that certainly makes sense to me, it is still not conclusively proven. Archeology is still very much on top of this issue. I could go on and on about this, but this is not the book for that.

By far the greatest threat to the Israelites was the Canaanite religion and its ever-present theological threat. As much as the Israelites tried to resist, the Canaanite religion would either seep into the Hebrew faith in covert ways, OR they were tempted to worship Canaanite gods outright. Israelites backslide time and time again to the religion of the Canaanites. Even when they emerged from it, Canaanite ideas were well transcribed into the DNA of Israelite religion. This is where Asherah comes in. Notice I do not call it Judaism. Judaism emerges from the Hebrew/Israelite faith but cannot really be called Judaism proper until much later. If you were to travel back in time and show the ancient Israelites the practices of Judaism, they would hardly recognize it. It is very different.

Israelite faith and later by extension, Judaism, at least **ON THE SURFACE,** does not have a divine feminine within its theological practices and beliefs. However, upon closer examination we find that they couldn't suppress the divine feminine completely. It was Asherah who emerged as consort to the Hebrew God. This is of course quite scandalous. Yet, some interesting evidence is present to suggest this.

A few books exist about Asherah, so I am going to jump in and add my two cents. I found the others to be rather complex. I will do my best to deconstruct it all in this book, but for the sake of brevity I can't go too deep. Like all my books, I will cover the texts and history. I have many old notes that I will clean up and present here.

We will discuss Asherah's wide-ranging presence from Akkadian sources all the way through Arabian ones and a few more. We will start with the Old Testament sources first since that is essentially what put her on the map of Intellectual history. We will also learn more about ways to call upon her and tap into her ancient power. She is after all, the divine consort of God, the Queen of the Heaven.

Asherah In the Old Testament

As I indicated in the introduction, Asherah is far more than a Canaanite Goddess. Her influence has been widespread throughout the Middle East and parts of North Africa. Although her cult was not as long-lived, as, let's say that of one of my patronesses, the great Goddess Isis of the ancient Egyptians. Her cult, however, was far more pervasive within the region than that of Isis. In many ways, the cult of Isis benefited from the attention she garnered from civilizations that appreciated her exoticism and Egyptian lore in general. Mainly, the Greeks and Romans, who of course, had the great ability to disseminate information across wide swaths of the Mediterranean and beyond, either by the pen or by the sword. It is for this reason you can find remnants of Isis cults as far away as Londinium (present-day London) via the Romans. The form found there, has only partial resemblance to her original form in Egypt; her cult was Hellenized. In essence, Asherah's cult was and remained regional, whereas the Isis cult went global.

Asherah's cult was not quite as exotic, for she, despite being Queen of Heaven, existed within a framework that did not distinguish her in ways that Isis was distinguished. This is partly because inscriptions of her are not as robust as that of Isis. There are many though. In addition, she would be, of course, later demonized by western religions because of her mention in the Bible. Isis was never directly mentioned in it, I am not even aware of even a hint of Isis in the Bible. This brings us to the topic at hand. In this chapter, we will discuss Asherah and her presence within the Old Testament tradition.

Chronologically, I should not start this book with Asherah's appearance in the Bible since her worship predated many biblical mentions of her I.e. via Ugaritic texts which we will discuss later. The reason I am starting with the Old Testament mention of her is because that is how most of us know about her. Asherah is featured quite a few times in the Old Testament. She was a thorn in the side of the Israelites. In the Old Testament, she is identified either directly by name or by her cult object the "Wooden Asherah Poles" or Asherim, Asherot and Ashteroth, which, by the way, is where the Goetia derived the demon name Ashteroth from. To be more precise, Asherah is mentioned 40 times in the Old Testament, of which 33 of those times appear to be referring to her by her sacred cult object. The fact she was often identified by these poles led many scholars to believe Asherah was not a Goddess but a description of a Pagan Cult Object. One of the reasons for this is due to the fact that we find mention of these poles using the word in Hebrew "Asherim", which is a plural word and used when referring to more than one of these poles. This theory was later abandoned when it was found in the Ugaritic texts that Asherah was, in fact, a prominent Goddess. We will look at a few passages in the Old Testament that indicate that she was a Goddess, but also some verses that also suggest a religious cult object.

I will supply both the English and Hebrew text of each verse I will mention in this text.

1 Kings 15:13:

"He also deposed his mother Maacah from the rank of queen mother, because she had made an abominable **thing for Asherah**…"

וְגַם אֶת־מַעֲכָה אִמּוֹ, וַיְסִרֶהָ מִגְּבִירָה, אֲשֶׁר־עָשְׂתָה מִפְלֶצֶת, לָאֲשֵׁרָה

This is an interesting passage, the word for "abominable thing" in Hebrew is "Meephletzet" מִפְלֶצֶת. This technically means a "Detestable Image" Or "Abominable Image". In modern Hebrew, this word also means *Monster.* Apparently, an image to Asherah was considered monstrous. Also notice that the letter Lamed before the Asherah indicates "FOR or TO" Asherah.

> וְגַם אֶת-מַעֲכָה אִמּוֹ, וַיְסִרֶהָ מִגְּבִירָה, אֲשֶׁר-עָשְׂתָה מִפְלֶצֶת, לָאֲשֵׁרָה

I mention this because this indicates that in this verse she is referred to as an individual being.

We find another in 2 Kings 21:7. It states, **"And he set the graven image of Asherah,** that he had made, in the house of which the LORD said to David and to Solomon his son: 'In this house, and in Jerusalem, which I have chosen out of all the tribes of Israel, will I put My name forever"

> ז וַיָּשֶׂם, אֶת-פֶּסֶל הָאֲשֵׁרָה אֲשֶׁר עָשָׂה--בַּבָּיִת, אֲשֶׁר אָמַר יְהוָה אֶל-דָּוִד וְאֶל-שְׁלֹמֹה בְנוֹ, בַּבַּיִת הַזֶּה וּבִירוּשָׁלִַם אֲשֶׁר בָּחַרְתִּי מִכֹּל שִׁבְטֵי יִשְׂרָאֵל, אָשִׂים אֶת-שְׁמִי לְעוֹלָם.

The first arrow on the left is pointing to the name Asherah and the one to the right is pointing to the letter HEI. In this case, the actual translation of this word would be "THE ASHERAH". Some have used this as evidence that it wasn't a singular Goddess per se, but a kind of Goddess or a kind of "Cult Object" since it does not refer to her as an individual entity, as in the previous verse. This can also be found with Lilith. Some texts refer to her as LILIM or Lilin. This word is plural and indicates a kind of class of

Lilith-like entities. In Ancient Babylon, the Lilitu was a class of entities.

In the next verse of 2 Kings, we find her being referred to more as a Goddess. It also mentions her consort Baal.

2 Kings 23:4

<u>all the vessels that were made for Baal, and for Asherah</u>, and for all the host of heaven..."

אֵת כָּל־הַכֵּלִים הָעֲשׂוּיִם לַבַּעַל וְלָאֲשֵׁרָה וּלְכֹל צְבָא הַשָּׁמָיִם

The red arrow is pointing to "To Asherah" and the Yellow arrow says, "To Baal". This verse is clear indication that Asherah is a spiritual being and a Goddess. The other interesting part of this verse is that after Asherah is mentioned it states, **"and for all the hosts of heaven"**. This implies that not only Baal and Asherah are divine, they are also part of the hosts of heaven. Interesting word usage by the biblical writer don't you think?

In **1 Kings 18:19** it states, "Now therefore send, and gather to me all Israel unto mount Carmel, **and the prophets of Baal four hundred and fifty, and the prophets of the Asherah four hundred,** that eat at Jezebel's table."

יט וְעַתָּה, שְׁלַח קְבֹץ אֵלַי אֶת-כָּל-יִשְׂרָאֵל--אֶל-הַר הַכַּרְמֶל; וְאֶת-נְבִיאֵי הַבַּעַל אַרְבַּע מֵאוֹת וַחֲמִשִּׁים, וּנְבִיאֵי הָאֲשֵׁרָה אַרְבַּע מֵאוֹת, אֹכְלֵי, שֻׁלְחַן אִיזָבֶל.

First highlight is "The prophets of The Baal" and the one other one is "The prophets of The Asherah".

Let us look at one more verse and then we will move on.
The following verse again will use Asherah's name, and Baal's for that matter as plural.

Judges 3:7 "And the children of Israel did that which was evil in the sight of the LORD, and forgot the LORD their God, and served **the Baalim and the Asheroth.**"

וַיַּעֲשׂוּ בְנֵי-יִשְׂרָאֵל אֶת-הָרַע בְּעֵינֵי יְהוָה, וַיִּשְׁכְּחוּ אֶת-יְהוָה אֱלֹהֵיהֶם; וַיַּעַבְדוּ אֶת-הַבְּעָלִים, וְאֶת-הָאֲשֵׁרוֹת.

The arrow to the left is pointing to "The Asherot" and the right arrow is pointing to "The Baalim". This literally means the Asherah's and the Baal's, as if they were class of being. Another explanation is that they were referring to variants of Asherah and Baal that were present throughout the region. Not all cultures and locales who worshiped Baal and Asherah did so in the same way. Even the names were slightly different in some instances, but they were still recognized as Baal and Asherah.

For example, we have Baal-Peor or the "Baal" of Peor" which, as a side note, is where the demon name Belphegor comes from. We also have Baal Zevuv, known in English as Beelzebub, which means "Lord of the flies" or literally "BAAL OF FLIES" etc. Some have suggested because the Hebrews did not consider these deities as being anything more than idols, they objectified them with **"THE"** as if they were an object. But as we have seen, there was also reference **"TO"** Asherah as well. Since we already know that Baal was, a God in a few mythological texts, having Asherah's name show up with his indicates she too is a Goddess.

Another way Asherah was identified was by her cult object which I hinted at earlier. Often one of the plurals of Asherah's name, Asherim would also refer to a grove or a kind of tree and in some cases, a manmade cult object or "Wooden Asherah

Pole". Here are a few examples of this in the Old Testament. I will first present it in English and then in Hebrew.

1 Kings 14:23

"For they also built them high places, and pillars, and Asherim, on every high hill, and under every leafy tree;"

וַיִּבְנוּ גַם-הֵמָּה לָהֶם בָּמוֹת וּמַצֵּבוֹת, וַאֲשֵׁרִים, עַל כָּל-גִּבְעָה גְבֹהָה, וְתַחַת כָּל-עֵץ רַעֲנָן.

In this example, you can see that It is clearly referring to an object. An object most associated with Asherah herself.

In the next verse, instead of using Asherim or Asherot as plurals of Asherah, it uses Asherah singular and uses language that objectified the name.

1 Kings 16:33

"And Ahab made **the Asherah**..."

There are a few more instances, but for the sake of brevity, let us move on.

Now that we have seen the distaste the biblical authors had for Asherah, let us look a bit more behind the scenes. The inscriptions I will discuss now are so controversial that I am shocked they aren't cited more often OUTSIDE of the Ivory Towers of Academia. I guess I could see why they would be ignored. It has the potential to upend the entire modern conception of the early Hebrew faith.

Before I go on, I would like to clarify one thing.

God in the Old Testament has several names, one of which is YHWH aka Yahweh. In fact, that is the main one, the "Tetragrammaton" as it is also known. It is often translated in English as "Lord".

The reason I mention this will be clear in a moment.

There was an ancient shrine found in the Sinai Peninsula, dating around the 9th to 8th century B.C. called Kuntillet Ajrud. They found an inscription in early Hebrew, but in Phoenician Script. Many inscriptions involve El, Baal and Asherah. The deities often associated with that general area. There is one more figure inscribed there as well, and that is YAHWEH and he is NOT alone. In fact, one inscription says **"Berahti ethem l'YHVH Shomron ul'Asherato"** in English, "I have blessed you by Yahweh of Samaria and his Asherah". As a side note, I pronounced the name YHVH as Yehovah because that is the most common way of pronouncing this name, if it is ever mentioned at all. The people who inscribed this may not have pronounced it that way.

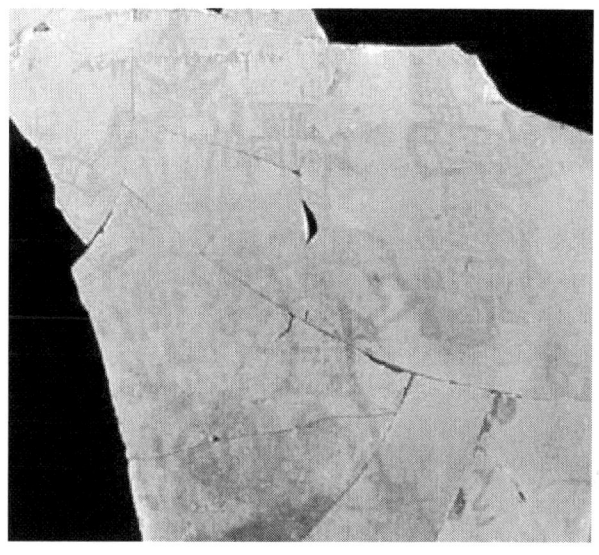

If you recall earlier, I quoted the O.T. illustrating that Ahab built an "Asherah". Well, this was the same period as the Kuntillet Ajrud inscriptions. It is clear she was incredibly popular during this period. There are other inscriptions that consistently associate Yahweh with Asherah as well. Many believe that during this time, Asherah was considered the divine consort and Queen to Yahweh. She was the only Goddess that the ancient Israelites really knew. In the book **'Gods, Goddesses and Images of God in Ancient Israel '** it states "Asherah was the only major Goddess surviving in Palestine".

In a great article in the Biblical Archaeology Review (September/October 2012) "**How the Mother God Got Spayed** "it states "Indeed, worship of the Mother God in conjunction with the Father God can be demonstrated to have occurred within ancient Israel. <u>Both the Bible and archaeology confirm this</u>. <u>So it isn't that the Mother God was absent from their worship. Rather she was consciously eradicated from worship by the religious authorities."</u> (http://members.bib-arch.org/biblical-archaeology-review/38/5/8).

Professor Oylan, A Brown University professor and author of "Asherah and the Cult of Yahweh" states:

"(The goddess Asherah) was an acceptable and legitimate part of Yahweh's cult in non-deuteronomistic circles. The association of the Asherah and the cult of Yahweh suggests in turn that Asherah was the consort of Yahweh in circles both in the north and the south (1988:33)."

Will Dever, the author of "Did God Have a Wife?" pretty much says the same thing. He mentions in the book that during archeological digs, many female figurines were found and that are part of Israelite folk religion or as Oylan called it "non-deuteronomistic circles", Yahweh was often depicted as having Asherah as a consort. She was known as the Queen of Heaven and during certain festivals, the Hebrews would bake cakes in her honor.

In light of this, we see that the prophet Jeremiah was talking about Asherah when he states in **Jeremiah 7:18:**

" **The children gather wood, and the fathers kindle the fire, and the women knead the dough, to make cakes to the Queen of Heaven..."**

We find further proof in the book of Jeremiah that many Israelites were nervous about NOT worshiping Asherah. They thought not doing so, brought upon them suffering.

Jeremiah 44:17-18 " **We will certainly do everything we said we would: We will burn incense to the Queen of Heaven and will pour out drink offerings to her just as we and our ancestors, our kings and our officials did in the towns of Judah and in the streets of Jerusalem. At that time, we had plenty of food and were well off and suffered no harm. [18] But ever since we stopped burning incense to the Queen of Heaven and pouring out drink offerings to her, we have had nothing and have been perishing by sword and famine."**

Those two verses are quite revealing, don't you think?

In later texts of Judaism, mainly the Talmud, Asherah is also mentioned, but within a legal text elucidating what is considered true idol worship as it pertains to Asherah poles or trees, amongst other practices. I will quote a passage here just to illustrate how the Rabbis processed these kinds of ideas.

In a Talmudic text called "Avodah Zarah" , which means, in English "Strange/foreign worship" or more the commonly , uninspired term "idolatry" it states the following:

"There are three laws of Asherot forbidden due to idolatry:

"If a tree was originally planted to be worshipped, it is forbidden;

If one cut it, leaving the stump or the branches in order to worship the new growth, if the new growth is removed, the tree is permitted;

If idolatry was put under it and removed it, the tree is permitted."

I know, it is rather "particular", the remainder of the text is just as convoluted, and more so. This particularity is common in the Talmud; it borders on the Compulsive. I will supply a link here for you to read the entire text of Avodah Zarah so you can get a full Talmudic experience as it pertains to Idol Worship.

Just an FYI, on the website below, the term for Asherot or plural of Asherah is Asheiros. This is simply a reflection of a European Jewish dialect (Ashkenazic) in which the Tav, the last letter of the Hebrew alphabet, is vocalized as an "S" and not a reference to a different goddess.

http://www.baalkadmon.com/asherahtalmud/

Asherah In the Ugaritic Traditions

Although we have quite a few references to Asherah in the Bible, her origin stories come from Ugarit.

We often see references to Ugaritic in discussions on the Old Testament and the archeology involving it. However, not many people get into what exactly this reference means. Ugarit was the Capital of a very prominent city-state in the Northwestern part of what is now, Syria. Ugarit is known now as Ras Sharma. It's texts have had much influence on the O.T. texts but mention of Ugarit itself is not present in the O.T. We do have reference to it in the Amarna Letters; these letters are correspondences between various Middle Eastern rulers and the Pharaoh/s of Egypt.

Ugarit would be dead to the ages if it was not for a peasant farmer who just happened to stumble upon it in 1928. Although we are mainly concerned with the inhabitants who lived in 2000-1200 B.C., the site itself is far older. Archeological evidence has found at least fifteen levels of human occupation in this area. Some of these settlements date as far back as 6000 B.C. and the most recent being the Early Roman period with a peak around 1500-1200 B.C. This peak is where we find most of the information we will need for our purposes.

In Ugaritic texts, she is known as ATRT pronounced Athirat. In some texts, she is referred to as "Ilit" which simply means Goddess. In many of the texts she is the consort of the God El or in Ugratic "IL" which simply means "God" this also holds true in Hebrew. El means God and can be found throughout the Old Testament in various forms. There is also evidence that she is the consort of the God Baal as well. We know this because it appears that she helps Baal in several instances.

One example is the story of Baal and his desire for a palace. He did not want the palace just for the sake of his ego. He wanted it as a reward for his defeat of the mighty sea God YAM, whose name literally means "sea". Defeating this sea monster conferred power and Baal earned his title to be King. There was only one problem, EL had to approve it. In the myth, another Goddess, Anat tries to intercede, but El refused her request for Baal to have a palace. However, Asherah - Athirat works her magick on El and he eventually acquiesces. This story can be found in what academic's call "The Baal Cycle", I will cover that in a future text.

In many of the myths revolving around her, she is portrayed in a very maternal light and will often come to the assistance of other deities as you have seen above. The discovery of archeology illustrating Asherah are not far and few between. Hundreds of Canaanite texts were found in Ugarit. She is shown in many of these texts to be the highest of all Goddesses before and during the emergence of the Hebrews/Israelites.

Some of the names ascribed to her are: The Queen of Heaven, Mother of the Gods, Lady Asherah, just to name a few. For the most part, prior to 1200 B.C., in most of the texts she is referred to as "Athirat Yammi" which literally means "Asherah of the Sea". This exact name appears a dozen times within the Baal Cycle stories. What's interesting about this name is that she is hardly ever really associated with the sea. So, I am not sure if we truly know why her name is associated with it. As I did mention before, Baal defeated the God Yam who was a sea God. Some evidence suggests that Asherah was on the side of of Yam, so perhaps that is why she acquired "sea" in her name. It is not uncommon to find multiple, contradictory stories in one tradition; we find countless contradictions within the biblical tradition. Another interesting name she has in Ugaritic is Caniyatu Ilhm which literally means creator of the Gods. Notice Ilhm and Elohim are very much the same word.

Clearly her role within Ugaritic traditions is more generative than it is in the Old Testament. She is a high goddess. She also appears in other traditions within the region as well. In the next chapter we will examine her appearance in the Ancient Egyptian tradition.

Asherah in Ancient Egypt

Ancient Egypt was arguably the most prominent nation in the Middle East and North Africa in ancient times. It has taken many hits over its nearly 3000-year history, but it has always either been on top or was, at the very least, the fascination of the known world. Another claim to fame for Egypt was the fact it was a net exporter of grain to the region, this was true right through late antiquity.

Part of Egypt's allure, aside from its monuments, was its religion. We know all the usual names: Osiris, Isis, Nephthys, Set, Horus, Ra, Bes, Bast and Sekhmet to name a few. There were many others in the pantheon that were lesser-known to the broader world but were still important. One of these was a Goddess by the name of Qudsu and other names that are variants of Qudsu, such as Kadesh, Qds etc.

Not much is known about her, but her name suggests that she has some Semitic roots. Another name also given to her is KADESH which as I mentioned above, as Quds, means holy in various Semitic dialects. She is often depicted very much like the Egyptian Goddess Hathor, standing between the Egyptian fertility God Min and the Semitic God Resheph. Although she looks like Hathor in the image below, the inscriptions say otherwise.

The inscriptions that are found under this image and others like it refer to her as "Queen of Heaven", "Mistress of Heaven", and "The Mistress of the Gods" and so forth. These names match Asherah's names in Ugaritic. Another clue that this might be Asherah is that one inscription says " Qudsu-Athirat-Anat". So, in essence, it is stating she is all three of these Goddesses. The

Stela in which this inscription is found has been used as evidence that this Qudsu figure is Asherah. I agree.

I don't see why this would not be the case. Both Egypt and Ugarit had a lot of exposure to one another and religious influences often flowed in both directions. The Amarna letters were proof of this.

Of course, not everyone agrees with me. Some say that due to this exposure, Gods and Goddess of varying cultures may often have similar iconography but not actually be the same God or Goddess. The one thing that I think gives it away that it is Asherah, is this... In Ugaritic texts, often Asherah's name is found parallel to **Qetesh** or Kadesh in the texts. I feel that this could be why the Egyptians referred to her as Qudsu as opposed to Asherah. I personally think it is Asherah. I will let the scholars in the Ivory towers of academia sort it... I am not holding my breath.

Asherah in Hittite Religion

Archeology may have many flaws, but the one thing it has illustrated time and time again, beyond a shadow of a doubt is that nations that are found in the same geographical area, tend to have many similar mythological and religious motifs. Even the names of the Gods are similar, if not exactly the same in some cases. This also applies to the religion of the ancient Hittites.

The Hittites were a very powerful civilization found in Ancient Anatolia or modern-day Turkey. Although they had a broad influence in the region, they are more popularly known as the nation who gave Egyptian Pharaoh, Rameses the II a run for his money at the Battle of Kadesh; a Battle that ended in a stalemate. (Don't believe what the ancient Egyptians say). I will not get into the details of the battle, but it is very interesting, and I suggest you research it. It is a battle that is still closely studied today in academia.

My apologies for the digression, let us get back to Hittite religion and Asherah.

In one myth, we have a God named Elkunirsha and his wife Ashertu; in their mythology, they easily correspond to the Canaanite God El and Asherah respectively. In this myth, we also find a storm God who would clearly correspond to Baal of the Canaanites.

In the Myth, we find that the storm God came to the "house" of Elkunirsha, it is there that Ashertu attempted to seduce him. He refused, and she threatened him. The storm God runs to Elkunirsha's tent in which he finds the God. Elkunirsha, in an interesting twist commanded that he go "lay" with Ashertu in order to "humble" her. Baal must have been quite some lover if his love was so humbling.

Well, the storm God acquiesces and has sex with Ashertu. While they are basking in the afterglow, the storm God whispers sweet nothings into her ear. He says, "I killed 77 of your 88 sons while on my way to you". The storm God sure is a romantic. I wonder if there is a Hallmark card that captures such a tender moment.

Although there is not much about her in this mythology, I did want to illustrate what we do know of her within it. Let us move on.

Asherah in Mesopotamia

Mesopotamia in its vastness contained many powerful and ancient cultures. One such ancient culture was the Akkadians. Akkad, aside from being a city, was also a catch all term for a region in Northern Mesopotamia.

Via Ugaritic texts, we find out that Asherah was known in Mesopotamia as Ashratum and Ashirta. We find cuneiform inscriptions of her dating to around 1800 B.C, in them, we find her to be the consort of the God Amurru. In the 14th century B.C, we even have a king with her name incorporated into his, a practice that was not uncommon in the region. The king's name was Amurru Abdi-Ashirta which means" Amurru, servant of Ashirta".

Even more ancient than this, she is mentioned in an inscription of Hammurabi, the great Babylonian law maker as "The Daughter-in-law of Anu" the great God of the Babylonians. She was also called "Belit Seri" which can be loosely translated as "Lady of the Steppes". Another name of hers which I feel embodies her power is "the mistress of fullness and abundance who is rightly honored in the mountains, mistress of mercy".

As I mentioned, often we find similar stories within the same region and therefore we should not be surprised that in both Ugarit and Mesopotamia, Asherah is often paired off with a God whose main animal symbol is the bull.

Now that we see she was also in Mesopotamia, let us look to see Asherah in Arabia.

Asherah in Arabia

This will be one of the shorter chapters since there isn't a lot of evidence for Asherah in Arabia, but I figured I would add this for your information.

In 1883, a stele was discovered in Northwestern Arabia. Most date it to around 550 B.C. The inscription is very clear and appears to be a list of Gods that appear to be local in nature, local to that area that is. There were a few names, one of which was Ashira. It is believed that the name Ashira is an Arabian inflection for the name Athirat from Ugarit or Asherah in Hebrew - **Baruch Margalit, "The Meaning and Significance of Asherah,"** *Vetus Testamentum* **40 (July 1990): 264–97.**

Asherah in Phoenicia

Ancient Phoenician tradition has many parallels to Canaanite traditions. In hindsight it is obvious why, but back when I was first starting out, it was not clear to me. I came to learn the similarities in an indirect manner. Phoenicia is an ancient Semitic civilization which comprised what we now know as Southwest Turkey, Lebanon, Syria, Israel and Gaza. It is their alphabet which is the predecessor to Hebrew. It had several colonies throughout the Mediterranean. Our attention will focus on one of these colonies, Carthage. Although technically in Tunisia, it was a Phoenician colony.

Since Ancient History is one of my specialties; one of my Masters degrees is in Ancient History, I have studied extensively such figures such as the great Carthaginian General and warrior Hannibal Barca, a man who was a huge headache for the Romans, but was ultimately defeated by them. If you look at Hannibal's name, we see indication of this Canaanite connection. His name means "Grace of Baal" or "Baal's Grace". We also learn that he performed blood sacrifices very early in his life to Baal Hammon. It is within this Carthaginian context that we will discuss the Asherah connection.

Some Say Asherah is the Goddess Tinnit or the more popular pronunciation Tanit, I will use Tinnit and Tanit interchangeably.

Some have said that she could also be the Goddess Anat. We can't know for sure, but I will include this anyway since, as we saw earlier, Anat and Asherah were considered one and the same in the Egyptian Qudsu inscription, and since Carthage is Egypt's next-door neighbor, this doesn't seem like such a stretch, at least not to me it doesn't. (Ok, they were about 1400 miles apart, but by this time it was quite easy to travel between Carthage and Egypt by sea. All you needed to do is hug the coast and you were there.)

Another reason why I say that Asherah might be Tanit is that in Punic (Carthaginian language also known as Phoenicio-Punic) it states that Tinnit is consort to Baal Hammon. If you recall earlier in the book, I mentioned that Baal often took on different names such as Baal Peor, Baal Zevuv (Beelzebub) etc. In the Latin texts that discuss the Punic wars, Baal Hammon was called a *"deus frugum"* Which means *'God of Fruit or Produce'*, which indicates he might have been a fertility God. Baal in other areas of the region was also a fertility god as well, in addition to being a storm god.

As we have seen earlier in the book, Asherah and Baal often show up together and thus, I believe that Tanit is Asherah.

With this chapter, we have concluded the history of the Asherah sightings in near eastern. I know I covered it broadly; I did this for the sake of brevity. If you would like to learn more about the archeology surrounding Asherah, I will provide resources at the end of the book.

In the next chapter, we will briefly discuss Canaanite religion in general and then we will jump into the ritual portion of this book.

Canaanite Religion in Brief

As I indicated earlier in the book, many of the Gods of the Canaanites were worshiped elsewhere in the Middle East; Such as Baal, El and Asherah as we have seen. The religion itself has always been shrouded in mystery. What we have in the Bible, although interesting, has a clear bias as we have seen.

When the texts of Ugarit were found, it shed new light on murky waters. We learn several things about the Gods in the Canaanite Pantheon.

Although the mythology of the Canaanites was "primitive" compared to its neighbors, we do find that the Gods therein had complex and dynamic personalities. I won't mention all of them, just those most pertinent to our discussion.

As in the Bible, a common word for the name of God was EL. As in the Bible, EL was considered the "God". It was only later in the Bible when his name was given suffixes like Shaddai, Elyon, etc. In Canaanite religion, EL was "the" name. He was the mighty one. EL had it pretty good, he had three wives, one we have met, Asherah, also known as illat which is just a feminine form of the name EL, the others are Anat and Astarte. Astarte is often confused with Asherah, but they are, in fact, different Goddesses. By the way, El is where we get the original concept of what god "looks" like. In Canaanite religion, he is described as a kindly looking old man with gray hair and a beard. Despite his status in the Heavens, he was not as popular as the God Baal.

Baal was central in Canaanite religion and was considered the King of the Gods. Despite him not being as "powerful" as EL, he was certainly more popular and much more widely worshiped. He also had a dynamic personality that stogy old EL seemed to lack. The relationship between Baal and El was a complex one. Despite El being the "Chief God", Baal does knock him off his perch and eventually takes over the reins of Heaven. Some scholars indicate that this story of Baal's defeat of El is illustrating a shift in the internal religious ideologies of the Canaanite religion. This, to me, is highly plausible. We also can see this kind of thing in other texts of the area. In the Old Testament, there is a VERY peculiar passage in which God speaks to Moses regarding his "name". Let's take a look. I will read it first in English and then Hebrew.

Exodus 6:2-3

" And God spoke unto Moses, and said unto him: 'I am the LORD, and I appeared unto Abraham, unto Isaac, and unto Jacob, as **God Almighty**, but by My name **YHWH** I made Me not known to them."

ב וַיְדַבֵּר אֱלֹהִים, אֶל-מֹשֶׁה; וַיֹּאמֶר אֵלָיו, אֲנִי יְהוָה.

ג וָאֵרָא, אֶל-אַבְרָהָם אֶל-יִצְחָק וְאֶל-יַעֲקֹב--בְּאֵל שַׁדָּי; וּשְׁמִי יְהוָה, לֹא נוֹדַעְתִּי לָהֶם.

In the second sentence, the first word in yellow "EL" second is Shaddai, which means almighty. So, the name here is "EL SHADDAI" or God Almighty. The name in orange is YHVH or Yahweh or The Tetragrammaton as it is more popularly known in Occult circles.

What the passage is saying is that to the early patriarchs, God appeared to them as a variant of EL and now his name is YHVH. Scholars say this indicates a shift in the theology of the Hebrews. So, in a long-winded way, what I am saying is that we see that EL is also supplanted in the Canaanite religion by Baal, who coincidently is the O.T. God's, greatest enemy. We know this because it was Baal's cult that caused the most grief for the Israelites. This is not to say that the name EL in both religions simply ceases to be mentioned, but rather they are no longer emphasized, indicating a break from the old. The Canaanites and Israelites were living side-by-side, so this similarity is not surprising.

Baal, as I mentioned, was the superstar of Canaanite religion. He wore many hats. He is the God of Fertility, of Storms, God of Justice and the Hater of Evil, Lord of Heaven, The Exalted one of the earth, the one who prevails. It was said that his kingdom was " Eternal to all generations". He was, in essence, the power behind all natural phenomena.

As with most mythological systems, the Canaanites considered the Gods and Goddesses to be inextricably linked to natural phenomena. Each God and Goddess represented the forces of nature. This also included the celestial bodies as well. Despite what you might have been told, this region of the Middle East is not always a hot desert. It too has seasons, in some places it snows, I have witnessed this myself. The Canaanites, as pretty much every mythological system portrayed the change of seasons as battles between the various Gods with one another. For example, during the dry season in which there is no rain, it was considered the death of Baal, a death brought on with his battle with the God of death, Mot.

When the rains did eventually come, it was considered not just Baal's resurrection so to speak, but also the sexual union between Baal and the Goddess Anat. These supernatural events were often reenacted ritually by the followers of Baal and the other Gods and Goddesses. This, of course, is very common. I can't think of one mythological system in which these seasonal rites were not enacted in some way. Sacred, sexual orgies were common during this time and were certainly not unique to the Canaanites.

Speaking of sacred sexuality, the Goddesses in Canaanite religion, mainly Asherah, Astarte and Anat were considered "Holy Sacred Prostitutes". Even their statuary would portray them with overt sexual details and they were most often portrayed naked. Such statues were found in the ruins of a temple located in North Israel, in a place called Beit She'an. I have been there personally and found the place dreadfully desolate. Aside from amazing archeological sites, nothing else really caught my eye. Of course, that was many years ago, and I am sure it has since changed.

Finding naked Goddess statues, of course, also indicates these are fertility Goddesses as well. Interestingly enough, it is found that these Goddesses were also war-like. Anat and Astarte for example were known to be blood thirsty in battle as well. It takes the adage " All's fair in love and war" to new dimensions...literally. It was not enough to simply worship these Gods and Goddesses, they also demanded sacrifice. This, of course, is common amongst every single religion of this time, including Hebrew religion. There are more mentions of Blood Sacrifices in the Bible than in any other text found in the region, so we shouldn't be surprised to hear this.

That in a nutshell is a description of some of the elements of Canaanite religion, AND it is the end of our historical analysis. We will now proceed to the ritual portion of this book.

Asherah and Her Ways

In this book, we will be calling upon Asherah for the following:

1. We will call upon her to vanquish our enemies.

2. We will Use Her to Attain Love.

3. To Gain Seductive Powers

4. We Will Call Upon Her For Abundance.

5. We Will Call Upon Her For Healing.

Much of the wording we will use in the Asherah rituals will be extracted and adapted from original Canaanite and Ugaritic texts.

Although these rituals will not be complicated, I do recommend that you get some form of representation of Asherah. I have one Asherah pole I use for rituals, someone made it for me. I am having another one made that will be five feet tall. I can't wait to see the finished product. If making an Asherah pole is too cumbersome, you may purchase a small statue from Amazon. It is in limited supply, when I purchased mine, there was only three left. I am hoping by the time you read this, they will be available.

You can, of course, print an image of Asherah off the web and perhaps fasten it to a branch or piece of wood to "mimic" an Asherah pole, this will be fine if it is not feasible to get or create an Asherah pole or statue.

As with all the rituals to Asherah, we must make an offering. Unlike many of Canaanite Gods, Asherah's main offering has been Wine or Water, Incense and or Cakes. We will incorporate one or more of these elements into to the rituals below. In terms of the kind of cake to use, I tend to use pound cake in a pinch, a single slice is fine. It would be best if you could bake a small cake for her, this will show much respect. If you can't bake it, pound cake is fine or any cake you like.

In the following chapters, we will cover the rituals. I will dedicate a chapter to each ritual for easy reference. Let us proceed.

Ritual – 1 - For Destruction of Your Enemies

1. In the center of the Altar, place the Asherah pole or Image of Asherah.
2. On one side, place a black candle, does not matter which side.
3. On the other side, place the incense. Please make sure the incense you use is one you very much like. We want to show respect to the Goddess; **any old incense will not do.**
4. Place the Cake offering right in front of the Asherah Pole or image.
5. Since this ritual is to destroy your enemies, please think of the person or persons who are wishing you harm. Even if the thought of them makes you tremble, this is okay, think of them. We will call upon Asherah to subdue them. If you have a picture of them, that would be even better. Please place under the image of Asherah.
6. Say the following:

"Oh Great Asherah, the warrior and Queen of Heaven, I ask that you, oh Great Lady, the great lady who trampled upon Yam, the God of the sea, come and trample upon those that wish harm upon me. Make

their feet to tremble, make their tendons to snap about them. Make their faces to sweat upon the thought of me. May their shame consume them from within. May you implore your heavenly council to assist you in this task. May it be so. Amen"

7. Sit for a moment and let Asherah permeate your space. Feel her energy around you. She is there.
8. Lift the piece of cake and pronounce the **name Asherah three times**. Eat a piece of the cake to imbibe a part of her.
9. Thank Asherah in your own words. It must be sincere.
10. Thus concludes the ritual.

The rest of the cake should be discarded in nature. Please allow the candle and incense to burn until completion. You will not need to do this ritual again, once is enough. You can make this ritual as long or as short as you like. I tend to go through it quickly in the book, but I have prolonged many rituals to an hour or more. Once the candle and incense are burned fully, you may return your altar to whatever configuration you had it originally.

Ritual – 2 – To Attain Love

1. In the center of the Altar, place the Asherah pole or Image of Asherah.
2. On one side, place a red candle, does not matter which side.
3. On the other side, place the incense. Please make sure the incense you use is one you very much like. We want to show respect to the Goddess; **any old incense will not do.**
4. Place the Cake AND wine/water offering right in front of the Asherah Pole or image.
5. Since this ritual is to attract love. Please think of the person you desire. If it is for a person you know, please write their name on a piece of paper. OR if you have a picture that would be even better. **(If it is for a specific person, the ritual will involve an additional step).** If this is not for a specific person, think of what it is you want to attain by performing this ritual. Once you have sufficient feeling and intent, please say the following.
6. **Say the following:**

    "**Oh Great Asherah, Queen of Heaven and ensnarer of the heart of mankind. Goddess of Love and Passionate lust, shower upon me your blessings and hear my** prayers. May it be so that I may find the love of my life, a love that burns as brightly as your love for Baal. Make the object of my desire pursue me as the great Gods of heaven pursued you. "

7. If this is for a specific person, take a sterile pin and prick your finger ever so lightly and smear a drop of your blood on the name or image of the person. **IF THIS IS NOT SOMETHING YOU FEEL COMFORTBLE WITH EITHER BECAUSE OF HEALTH REASONS OR OTHER, YOU MAY USE A DROP OF SALIVA.**
8. Sit for a moment and let Asherah permeate your space. Feel her energy around you. She is there.
9. Lift the piece of cake and pronounce the **name Asherah three times**. Eat a piece of the cake to imbibe a part of her. Now Take the water and or wine and drink it. Please be responsible if it is wine. *If you should not be drinking alcohol, use water.*
10. Thank Asherah in your own words. It must be sincere.
11. Thus concludes the ritual.

The rest of the cake should be discarded in nature. Please allow the candle and incense to burn until completion. **You should not do this ritual more than three times in one month**. Chances are, you won't need to do it more than once. You can make this ritual as long or as short as you like. Once the candle and incense are burned fully, you may return your altar to whatever configuration you had it originally.

Ritual – 3 – To Gain Seductive Power

1. In the center of the Altar, place the Asherah pole or Image of Asherah.
2. On one side, place a red candle and black candle, does not matter which side they are on.
3. On the other side, place the incense. Please make sure the incense you use is one you very much like. We want to show respect to the Goddess; **any old incense will not do.**
4. Place the Cake AND wine/water offering right in front of the Asherah Pole or image.
5. Since this ritual is to gain seductive power, I suggest you dress in a way that makes you feel sexy. Put on a perfume or cologne you like. You want to be " In the mood". If you need to be naked, BE NAKED. Do whatever it is you need to do to feel seductive.
6. **Say the following:**
7. **"Oh Great Asherah, Queen of Heaven and sacred prostitute of the temple. You are beautiful and your eyes are like doves, you are truly beautiful. No one can compare to you, Queen of Heaven. You are like a Lily in the brambles, none are like you. No one can or dares say no to you. As your servant, I ask you to**

bestow the same power over men/women that you have over the hosts of heaven and earth. Make them look upon me with lust and passion, as Baal, El and Yahweh look upon you. Allow me to be as a glistening jewel that no one can resist. I know this shall be done. Amen Selah."

8. Think for a moment what it would be like to be seductive. Sit with this feeling. Smell the cologne or perfume you are wearing. Look at yourself in the mirror and feel seductive.
9. Sit for a moment and let Asherah permeate your space. Feel her energy around you. She is there inside of you.
10. Lift the piece of cake and pronounce the **name Asherah three times**. Eat a piece of the cake to imbibe a part of her. Now Take the water and or wine and drink it. Please be responsible if it is wine. *If you should not be drinking alcohol, use water.*
11. Thank Asherah in your own words. It must be sincere.
12. Thus concludes the ritual.

The rest of the cake should be discarded in nature. Please allow the candle and incense to burn until completion. **Do this ritual as often as you like or when you feel you need to turn on the charm so to speak.** Chances are, you won't need to do it more than once. You can make this ritual as long or as short as you like. Once the candle and incense are burned fully, you may return your altar to whatever configuration you had it originally.

Ritual – 4 – We Will Call Upon Her For Abundance

1. In the center of the Altar, place the Asherah pole or Image of Asherah.
2. On one side, place a gold candle, does not matter which side it is on.
3. On the other side, place the incense. Please make sure the incense you use is one you very much like. We want to show respect to the Goddess; **any old incense will not do.**
4. Place the Cake in front of the Asherah Pole or image.
5. Since this ritual is to attain abundance, think of the type of abundance you require. Abundance can be more than just money.
6. Say the following:
7. **"Oh Great Asherah, Queen of Heaven and provider to all of heaven and earth and to your servants, I call upon you to bestow upon me the abundance and prosperity I so require. Your deeds are known to all, you are the faith and trust of the entire world. You cause the earth to overflow in abundance , your greatly enrich it. You are fertile with the abundance of all life. I am here, before you, asking for a small portion of this abundance. I will be forever grateful**

and will praise your name to ends of the earth. Bestow upon me your riches. Amen "

8. Think for a moment what this abundance will mean to you. Is it only for money? If so, how will you live with this abundance? It is important to have powerful intent.
9. Sit for a moment and let Asherah permeate your space. Feel her energy around you.
10. Lift the piece of cake and pronounce the **name Asherah three times**. Eat a piece of the cake to imbibe a part of her..
11. Thank Asherah in your own words. It must be sincere.
12. Thus concludes the ritual.

The rest of the cake should be discarded in nature. Please allow the candle and incense to burn until completion. **Do this ritual as often as you like . BUT do not do it in a spirit of desperation.** Chances are, you won't need to do it more than once. You can make this ritual as long or as short as you like. Once the candle and incense are burned fully, you may return your altar to whatever configuration you had it originally.

One more thing, if she comes through for you, please publically praise her name and thank her for the assistance.

Ritual – 5 – We Will Call Upon Her For Healing

1. In the center of the Altar, place the Asherah pole or Image of Asherah.
2. On one side, place a green and yellow candle, does not matter which side they are on.
3. On the other side, place the incense. Please make sure the incense you use is one you very much like. We want to show respect to the Goddess; **any old incense will not do.**
4. Place the Cake in front of the Asherah Pole or image.
5. Since this ritual is to attain healing. Please focus on the part of you that needs healing most. Don't dwell on it but just think about it for a moment. Think of how it would be to be healed of it.
6. **Say the following:**
7. **"Oh Great Asherah, Queen of Heaven and provider to all and healer of the sick. You bless the food and water and remove disease from those who serve you. Today, I ask for your healing energy to remove sickness from my body and mind. Have compassion on me Queen of heaven, for I am weakened, heal me. I know that all you must do is send out the word and I will be healed. You can restore my health and allow**

me to live. Do this for me, and I will praise your name to the four corners of the earth. You are the healer of the healers. Amen Selah"

8. Think for a moment what it would be like to be healed and believe it will be so. Nothing is impossible for Asherah.
9. Sit for a moment and let Asherah permeate your space. Feel her energy around you.
10. Lift the piece of cake and pronounce the **name Asherah three times.** In this case, eat the entire piece of cake, it will be as a medicine.
11. Thank Asherah in your own words. It must be sincere.
12. Thus concludes the ritual.

Please allow the candle and incense to burn until completion. **Do this ritual as often as you like. If you rather use a 7 day candle and do this for seven days straight, you can do so as well.** You can make this ritual as long or as short as you like. Once the candle and incense are burned fully, you may return your altar to whatever configuration you had it originally.

If she comes through for you, please publically praise her name and thank her for the assistance. Also please let me know, I would be interested to hear your story... In confidence, of course.

Conclusion

There you have it my friends. Asherah, the Queen of Heaven. I personally love to work with Asherah and I feel you will find her energy new. She not like the others you may find that are more "popular".

I know the rituals are super easy, but if you have used the rituals in my other books, you know that less is more. There is no reason to complicate any of it.

I hope you enjoy this book. Please visit me at www.baalkadmon.com and learn about my latest works and courses. I hope to see you there.

So Mote It Be,

Baal Kadmon

www.baalkadmon.com

www.occultmindscapes.com

http://www.occultcoures.com

Additional Resources

Olyan, Saul M. (1988) *Asherah and the Cult of Yahweh in Israel.*

Dever, William G *Did God Have a Wife?: Archaeology and Folk Religion in Ancient   Israel.*

Biblical Archaeology Review

Cornelius, Izak (2004) The *Many Faces of the Goddess: The Iconography of the Syro-Palestinian Goddesses Anat, Astarte, Qedeshet and Asherah c. 1500-1000 BCE*

Day, John (1986) "Asherah in the Hebrew Bible and Northwest Semitic Literature," *Journal of Biblical Literature.*

Occult Courses

Over the years, I have received many hundreds of emails asking me if I would ever consider creating online video courses. At first, I was unsure. After so many emails, I decided it was time.

I am now offering courses.

If it interests you in learning more about the **Occult, Meditation, Ancient Languages and History**, you will not be disappointed.

All courses will all be accessible, informative and affordable.

Please go to www.occultcourses.com

There you will find my current courses and all the upcoming courses. If you see a current course you are interested in, you can sign up and get **instant access.**

If you see a future course that interests you, sign up to the mailing list and I will notify you upon its release.

All courses come with a **30-day, no questions asked, money-back guarantee**. If a course is not for you, just let me know, and I will refund you.

Please go to www.occultcourses.com

Want to Enhance Your Rituals?

I am not one to promote myself. I like to keep things low-key, but I created a new service that has proven to enhance your rituals and your state of mind and I am very excited about it. As many of you may know, I use Brainwave Entrainment Audios to enhance my writing, my rituals and a lot more. I have been using brainwave products since the 80s. I am using one now as I write this.

I have created hyper-specific Brainwave audios geared to specific spiritual entities. For example, if you call upon the demon, King Paimon, I have a specific audio for him. If you work with the Hindus Goddess Lakshmi, I have a Brainwave Audio for her as well.

Please visit: www.occultmindscapes.com

I am adding Audios every week and will have something for everyone and for every tradition. I am only charging $3.95 per audio MP3 download, with steep discounts for multiple purchases.

I think you will LOVE them. My beta testers loved them and I am confident you will find them useful as well.

About Baal Kadmon

Baal Kadmon is an Author, Occultist, and Meditation teacher based out of New York City. In addition to the Occult, he is a Scholar of Religion Philosopher, and Historian specializing in Ancient History, Late Antiquity and Medieval History. He has studied and speaks Israeli Hebrew, Classical Hebrew, Ugaritic language, Arabic, Judeo-Aramaic, Syriac (language), Ancient Greek and Classical Latin.

Baal first discovered his occult calling when he was very young. It was only in his teens, when on a trip to the Middle East that he heeded the call. Several teachers and many decades later he felt ready to share what he had learned.

His teachings are unconventional to say the least. In addition to rituals, he includes in depth history in almost all the books he writes. He shatters the beloved and idolatrously held notions most occultists hold dear. His pared-down approach to Magick and Meditation is refreshing and is very much needed in a field that is mired by self-important magicians and teachers who place more importance on pomp and circumstance, than on Magick and Meditation. What you learn from Baal is straight-forward, with no frills. There is no need to complicate things.

www.baalkadmon.com

www.occultcourses.com

www.occultmindscapes.com

Follow Him on Facebook and other Social Media Sites:

http://baalkadmon.com/social-media/

Other Books By The Author

Organized by date of publication from most recent:

Surya Mantra Magick (Mantra Magick Series Book 13)

Tiamat Unveiled (Mesopotamian Magick Book 3)

Pazuzu Rising (Mesopotamian Magick Book 2)

BAAL: THE LORD OF THE HEAVENS: CALLING DOWN THE GREAT GOD OF CANAAN (CANAANITE MAGICK Book 2)

Chod Practice Demystified: Severing the Ties That Bind (Baal on Buddhism Book 2)

The Talmud: An Occultist Introduction

The Path of the Pendulum: An Unconventional Approach

Durga Mantra Magick: Harnessing The Power of the Divine Protectress

Asherah: The Queen of Heaven (Canaanite Magick Book 1)

Dependent Origination for the Layman (Baal on Buddhism Book 1)

The Watchers And Their Ways

Rabbi Isaac Luria: The Lion of the Kabbalah (Jewish Mystics Book 1)

Circe's Wand: Empowerment, Enchantment, Magick

Ganesha Mantra Magick: Calling Upon the God of New Beginnings

Shiva Mantra Magick: Harnessing The Primordial

Tefillin Magick: Using Tefillin For Magickal Purposes (Jewish Magick Book 1)

Jesus Magick (Bible Magick Book 2)

The Magickal Moment Of Now: The Inner Mind of the Advanced Magician

The Magick Of Lilith: Calling Upon The Great Goddess of The Left Hand Path (Mesopotamian Magick Book 1)

The Magickal Talismans of King Solomon

Mahavidya Mantra Magick: Tap Into the 10 Goddesses of Power

Jinn Magick: How to Bind the Jinn to do Your Bidding

Magick And The Bible: Is Magick Compatible With The Bible? (Bible Magick Book 1)

The Magickal Rites of Prosperity: Using Different Methods To Magickally Manifest Wealth

Lakshmi Mantra Magick: Tap Into The Goddess Lakshmi for Wealth and Abundance In All Areas of Life

Tarot Magick: Harness the Magickal Power of the Tarot

The Quantum Magician: Enhancing Your Magick With A Parallel Life

Tibetan Mantra Magick: Tap Into The Power Of Tibetan Mantras

The 42 Letter Name of God: The Mystical Name Of Manifestation (Sacred Names Book 6)

Tara Mantra Magick: How To Use The Power Of The Goddess Tara

Vedic Magick: Using Ancient Vedic Spells To Attain Wealth

The Daemonic Companion: Creating Daemonic Entities To Do Your Will

Tap Into The Power Of The Chant: Attaining Supernatural Abilities Using Mantras (Supernatural Attainments Series

72 Demons Of The Name: Calling Upon The Great Demons Of The Name (Sacred Names Book 5)

Moldavite Magick: Tap Into The Stone Of Transformation Using Mantras (Crystal Mantra Magick Book 1)

Ouija Board Magick - Archangels Edition: Communicate And Harness The Power Of The Great Archangels

Chakra Mantra Magick: Tap Into The Magick Of Your Chakras (Mantra Magick Series Book 4)

Seed Mantra Magick: Master The Primordial Sounds Of The Universe (Mantra Magick Series Book 3)

The Magick Of Saint Expedite: Tap Into The Truly Miraculous Power Of Saint Expedite (Magick Of The Saints Book 2)

Kali Mantra Magick: Summoning The Dark Powers of Kali Ma (Mantra Magick Series Book 2)

Mary Magick: Calling Forth The Divine Mother For Help (Magick Of The Saints Book 1)

Vashikaran Magick: Learn The Dark Mantras Of Subjugation (Mantra Magick Series Book 1)

The Hidden Names Of Genesis: Tap Into The Hidden Power Of Manifestation (Sacred Names Book 4)

The 99 Names Of Allah: Acquiring the 99 Divine Qualities of God (Sacred Names Book 3)

The 72 Angels Of The Name: Calling On the 72 Angels of God (Sacred Names)

The 72 Names of God: The 72 Keys To Transformation (Sacred Names Book 1)

Made in the USA
Columbia, SC
10 July 2025